Returning to Joy

NASHVILLE

NEW YORK • LONDON • MELBOURNE • VANCOUVER

Returning to Joy

Inspiration for Grieving the Loss of Your Cat

Published in New York, New York, by Morgan James Publishing. Morgan James is a trademark of Morgan James, LLC. www.MorganJamesPublishing.com

ISBN 9781631954214 hardcover
ISBN 9781631954221 eBook
Library of Congress Control Number: 2020923037

Cover & Interior Design by:
Juliet Ekinaka,
Lunations, Inc

Morgan James is a proud partner of Habitat for Humanity Peninsula and Greater Williamsburg. Partners in building since 2006.

Get involved today! Visit
MorganJamesPublishing.com/giving-back

A MESSAGE FROM THE AUTHOR

I know grief—not because my life has been filled with sadness. On the contrary, it has been filled with love. Smoke was one of my life's great loves.

My cat and best buddy for twenty-two years, she was also the most beloved treasure of my husband, Bill. Smoke witnessed the highs and lows of my life. When I lost Bill and Smoke, I lost my entire family.

Through my grief, I have learned that gratitude brings healing, and I hope this book helps you find both.

-Kristi

To those who have loved and lost, to those who continue to love despite grief, and most of all, to my dear Smoke, whose friendship and love still mean the world to me.

CHANGED HEART

Your paw prints are forever engraved on my heart.

To grieve is to change. Grieving the loss of a beloved companion is a testament to the love you gave and the love you received.

When your sweet friend is no longer with you, the love you shared remains, imprinted on your forever-changed heart. Let the grief change you for the better.

THE ESSENCE OF WHO YOU ARE

You'll always be with me, curled up in the center of my soul.

Just as your cat lounged in your favorite chair or warmed up by the fireplace, they remain curled up in the center of your soul – like a tiny seed within an apple.

Their essence is part of you now. Embrace it. When you miss your friend, feel their presence, resting within your chest and warming your heart.

JOYFUL MEMORIES

When tomorrow starts without you, I'll look to your memory for comfort.

Your cherished pet was there in all the details of your life, rubbing your legs and contentedly purring through both the happiest and hardest times.

Memories may trigger feelings of grief, but they also recall moments of immeasurable joy. Cherish these memories and appreciate the joy they still bring you.

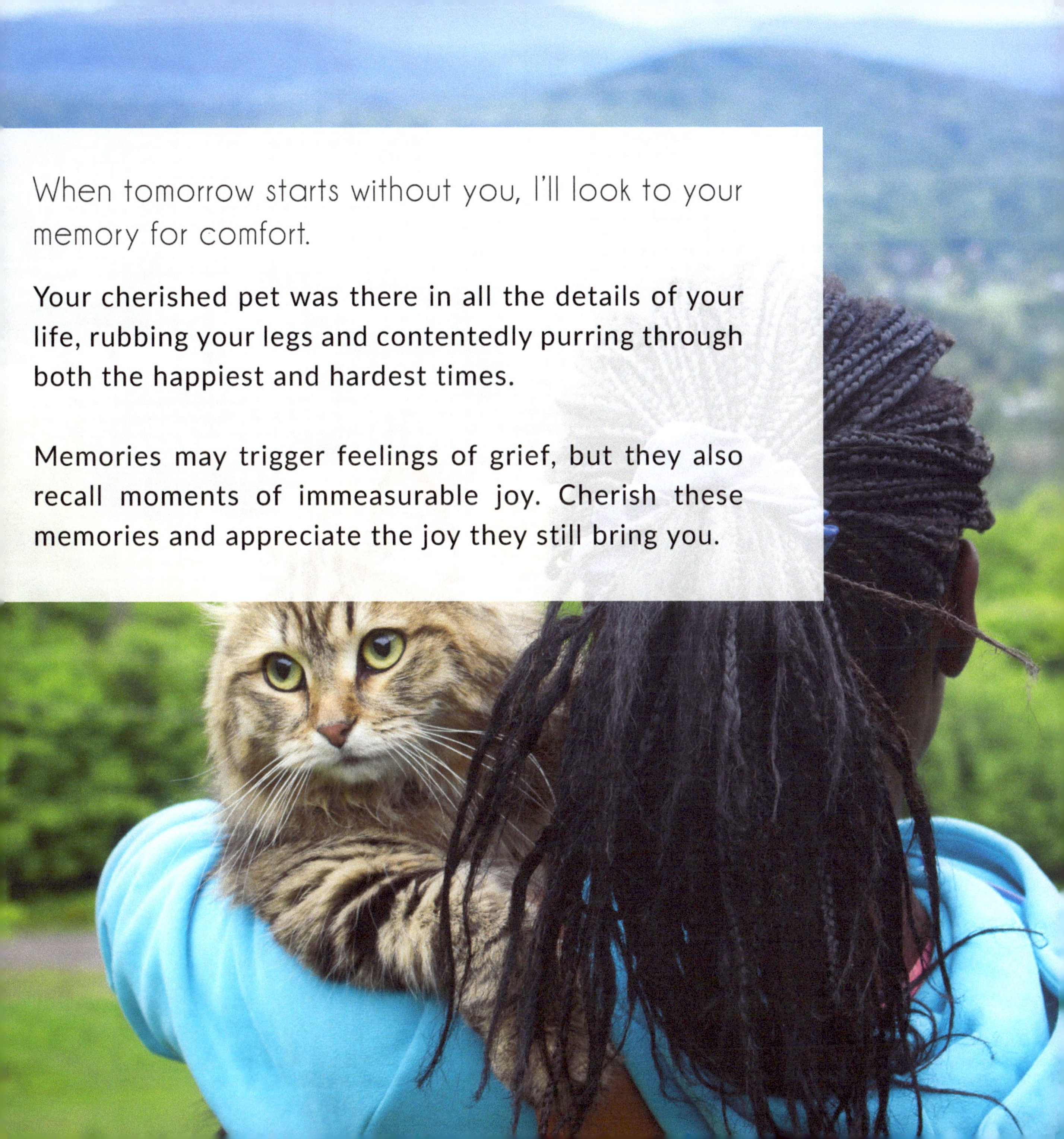

WINGS OF INDEPENDENCE

Your free spirit has given me wings.

Affectionate but independent, your sweet friend taught you a lesson in self-care. They followed their instincts, looking out for their own needs before pleasing others. Your cat marched to their own beat and respected their own boundaries. Let their free, independent spirit give you wings to trust yourself, care for your needs, and achieve your dreams.

SUN STILL SHINING

Behind the storm clouds, God's sun still shines.

"The light shines in the darkness, and the darkness has not overcome it."
John 1:5

Light cannot exist without shadows. Have faith in the divine, even when you feel stuck in the darkness of life. Light is powerful; it always breaks through.

Take a walk and appreciate the beauty of nature. Drink in fresh air and appreciate the complex, contradictory, and infinitely beautiful world God has created.

BREATHING JOY

Breathe in tears, breathe out joy.

"Blessed are you who weep now, for you will laugh."
Luke 6:21

Your thoughts, feelings, and emotions are inseparably connected, mingling with every breath. During your cat's life, your friend helped you stop and reflect, jumping on your lap for a moment of simple connection.

Honor their memory through moments of peaceful meditation each day.

Breathe through your grief, allowing the memories to wash over you in waves of sadness and joy.

THE FABRIC OF LIFE

You're woven into the fabric of my life.

A loyal pet shares your life journey — not as a spectator, but as a companion.

For that, your dear friend is more than a memory; they are tightly woven into the essence of your very being.

UNCONDITIONAL LOVE

I will forever be grateful for your gift of unconditional love.

"A friend loves at all times."
Proverbs 17:7

The most loyal friends accept you as you are – at your best as well as your worst.

Your sweet pet loved without judgment, teaching you the meaning of "unconditional." Let their example be your guide in loyalty and love.

A GIFT FROM GOD

I asked God, and I got you.

Your special pet was a gift from God – a kind and loyal companion to see you through the peaks and valleys of life. Just as God gave you this special gift, He's there now to help you through your loss. Put your trust in Him.

ANGELS WITH PAWS

"Are not all angels ministering spirits sent to serve those who will inherit salvation?"
Hebrews 1:14

Some angels have four paws.

Your dear friend taught you to love, laugh, and experience joy, how to curl on a couch and truly live in the moment. They were and remain a gift from heaven, living on in your memory.

GRATITUDE FOR EVERY MOMENT

I have gratitude for every moment I had with you.

As you grieve, recognize each moment you shared with your friend as a unique and beautiful gift. Reflect on your gratitude for the time you shared with your sweet cat.

Just as you savored those moments then, choose now to live in the present.

Appreciate the beauty of your past together, allowing this gratitude to shape your future.

WAITING AT THE DOOR

You're still there waiting at the door.

In life, doors constantly open and close. Opportunities open. Relationships close.

Just as they waited by the door for you to return home, your cat is waiting for you now.

Enjoy your life, knowing your sweet companion will be there to greet you when you open that final door.

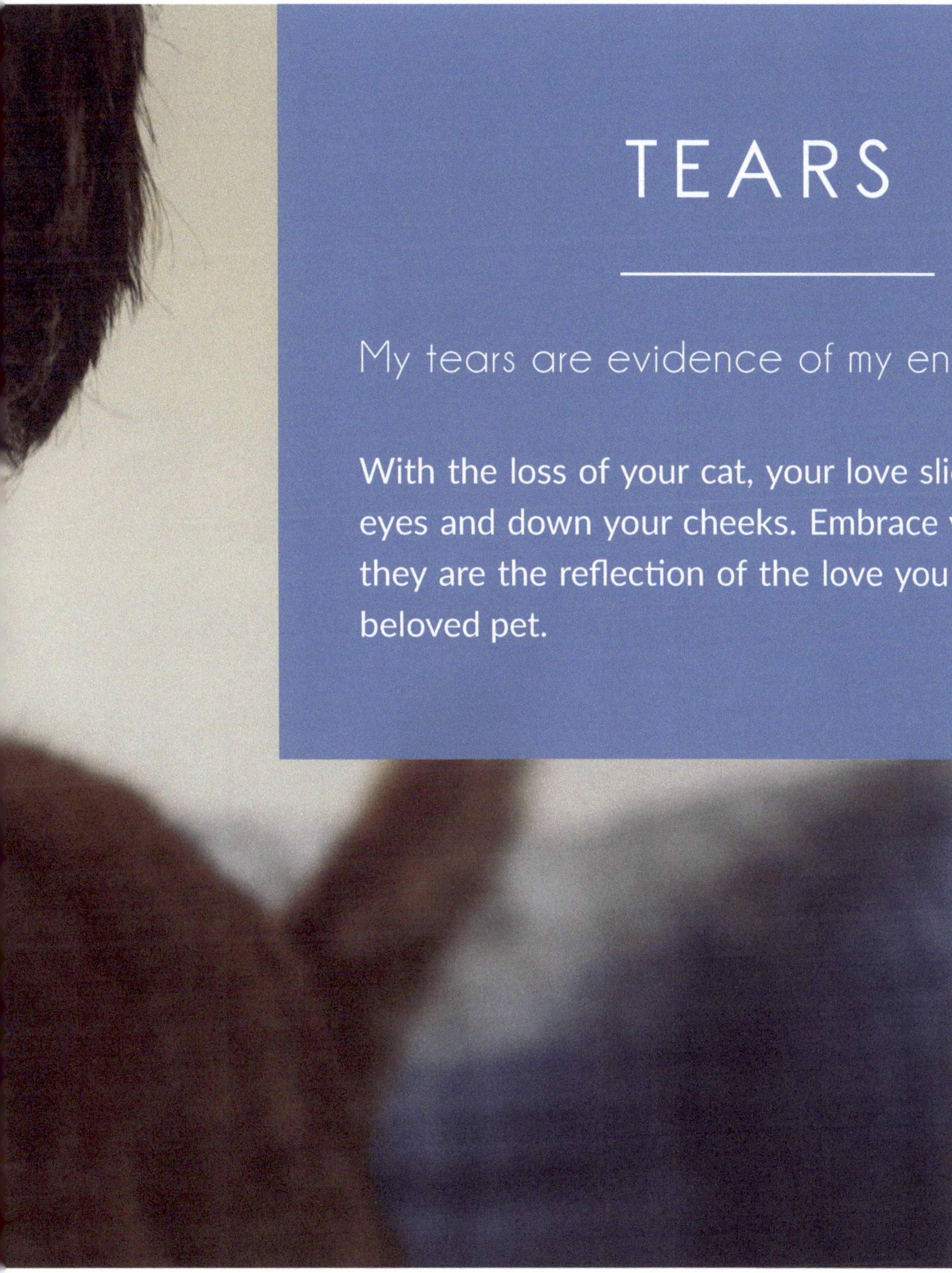

TEARS

My tears are evidence of my enduring love.

With the loss of your cat, your love slides from your eyes and down your cheeks. Embrace your tears, for they are the reflection of the love you have for your beloved pet.

GOD'S GRACE

"A cheerful heart is good medicine, but a crushed spirit dries up the bones."
Proverbs 17:22

My cat taught me God's grace.

Your dear friend made you a better person. In caring for them, you practiced generosity and love.

You fed, bathed, and nurtured your cat in sickness and health. Through this experience, you saw your pet as God sees you – a gift to love and care for. As you cared for your friend, let God care for you now.

LOVE THROUGH DARKNESS

The darkness of grief cannot extinguish the light of my love.

Grief can sometimes feel like an overwhelming darkness — a nighttime of the soul. But nothing can extinguish the deep love you shared with your feline friend.

Don't quiet your memories, however painful they may feel right now. These memories fan the flame of your everlasting love.

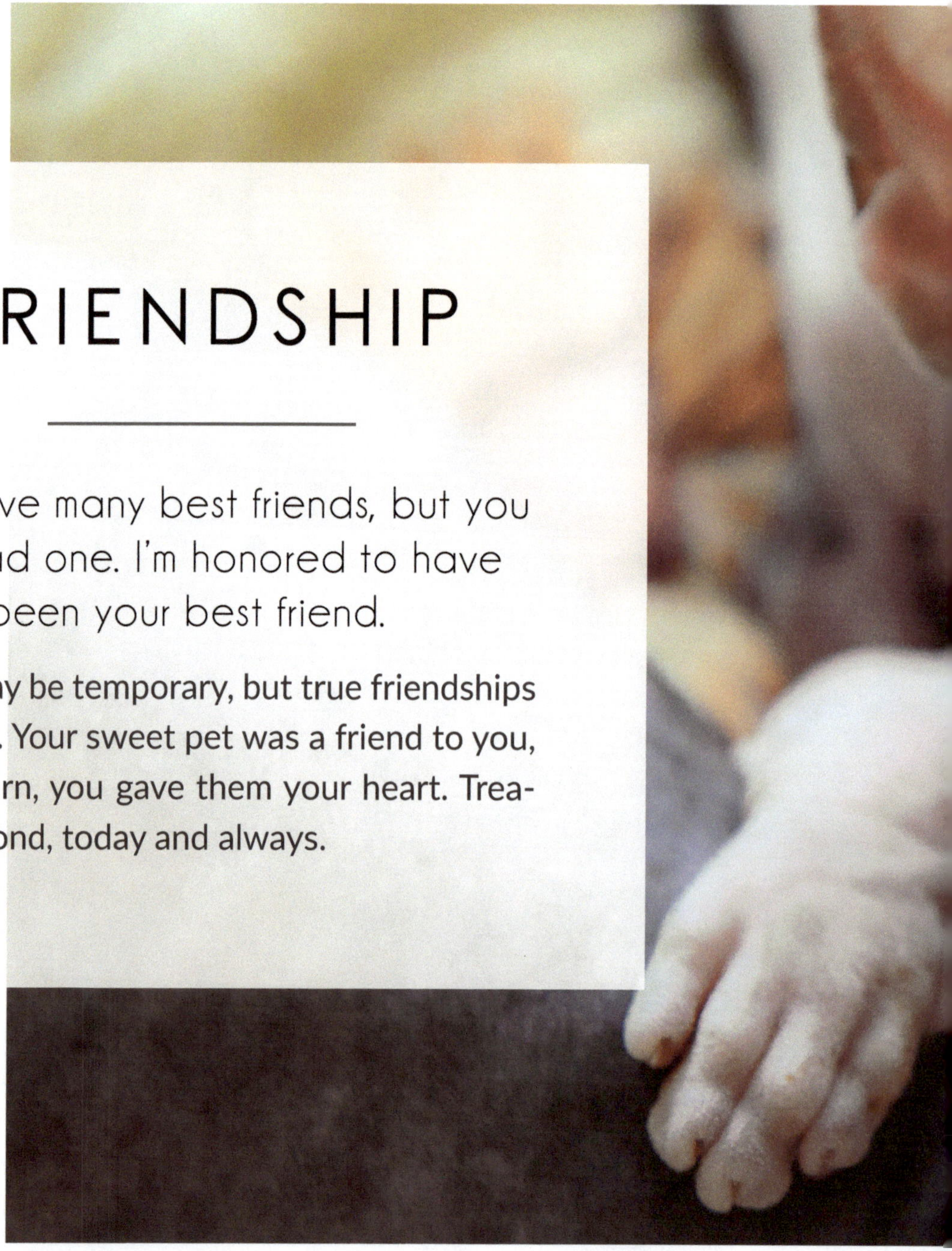

FRIENDSHIP

I may have many best friends, but you only had one. I'm honored to have been your best friend.

This life may be temporary, but true friendships are eternal. Your sweet pet was a friend to you, and in return, you gave them your heart. Treasure this bond, today and always.

FLEETING SUN RAYS

You were a fleeting sun ray, sent to brighten my days.

A cat's life is fleeting, destined to end before ours. To love a pet is to accept the inevitability of eventual loss — and keep loving anyway.

Knowing your earthly companionship was fleeting, you savored each moment you spent together. These memories are sun rays, too — eternal rays that can brighten your life forever if you let them.

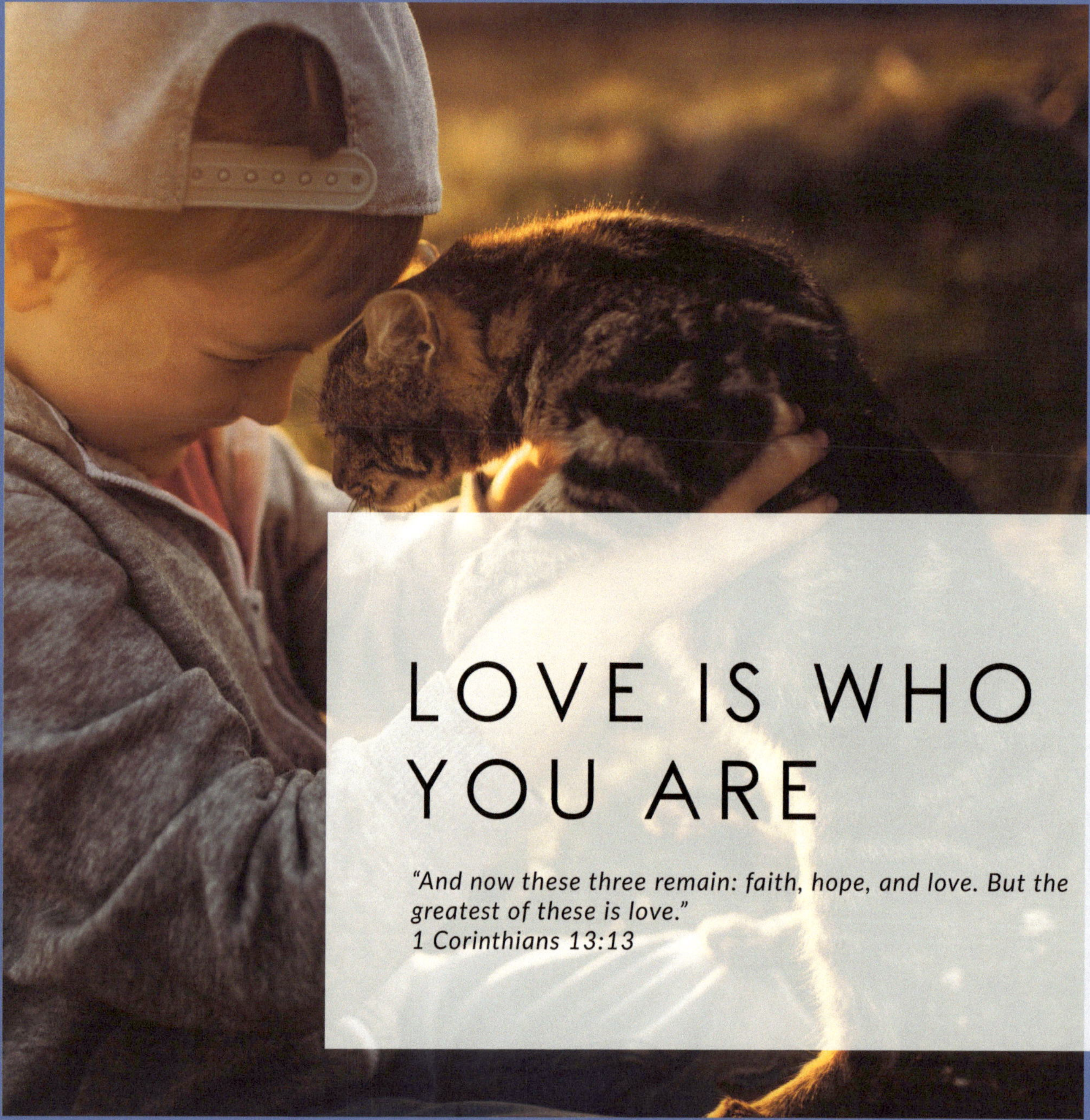

LOVE IS WHO YOU ARE

"And now these three remain: faith, hope, and love. But the greatest of these is love."
1 Corinthians 13:13

What I love is who I am.

Just as God loves His children, you loved your cat. Let that love reach every facet of your being, making you kinder and more understanding.

Through the demands of life, remember this love and how it has shaped who you are.

GRATITUDE IS ETERNAL

I am grateful for what was,
is, and will be.

"Give thanks in all circumstances."
1 Thessalonians 5:18

Gratitude is eternal.

To live with thanksgiving means recognizing your blessings – past, present, and future. While you grieve past memories, look forward to blessings yet to come.

Today, focus your faith on a future filled with love and happiness.

GRIEVE WITH GRACE

I will respect my grief with patience and care.

Grieving is not a linear process. You are suffering a great loss, and you can expect good days and bad days.

Be patient with yourself. Honor your grief by feeling it. And when good days come, allow yourself joy with the same grace you allow the pain.

TIME OF RENEWAL

My grief gives me an opportunity to renew myself.

Grieving a difficult loss inevitably changes you. Allow yourself to change and grow from this experience.

Explore new things, take up new hobbies, or meet new people. Remember, when you've been broken open, there are limitless opportunities for growth.

ROAD TO PEACE

My journey will take me through twists, turns, and tears. But I have faith it will lead me to peace.

"Blessed are those who mourn, for they will be comforted."
Matthew 5:4

Grieving is like climbing a mountain. Sometimes, the path is steep and rocky, and at times you may wonder whether you have the strength to go on. You may need to stop and catch your breath, but you keep going. And in doing so, you find out how strong you really are.

PERMISSION

"I waited patiently for the Lord; he turned to me and heard my cry."
Psalms 40:1

I will give myself permission to grieve.

As you grieve, you may feel the pressure to "get over it." Someone you love may even make you feel like your loss isn't worthy of grief.

Listen to your heart and allow yourself to feel. Your dear pet was a gift from God, a treasure for which you're forever grateful. Honor their memory as the blessing they truly were.

GRIEF CHANGES

My grief will change and so will I.

In the darkness of your grief, it's difficult to believe you'll ever feel differently. And while your grief won't disappear, it will change.

Embrace the journey, and welcome the changes you see within yourself.

GUARDIAN ANGEL

You are my guardian angel.

"For he will command his angels concerning you to guard you in all your ways."
Psalms 91:11

A loyal companion in this life, your sweet friend can never really be gone. Instead, they are in your heart and an inextricable part of your soul.

Allow yourself to believe your dear cat is with you, a guiding force and listening ear when times are hard.

LISTEN TO YOURSELF

I will listen closely to myself and my needs.

Candid in their feelings and needs, cats teach us to recognize and honor ours. Your sweet friend purred and played when they were happy, rested when they were sick, and retreated when they needed a moment alone.

Let this example inspire you in your own self-care. Listen closely to your feelings and show yourself the kindness and patience you deserve.

RESPECT YOUR GRIEF

My grief deserves respect and understanding.

Grief is complex, and your loss is anything but simple. You miss your dear friend, but you also miss the parts of yourself and your day that were tied to them, like reaching under the table to scratch their ears or feeling them hop onto your bed each morning. The loss you feel is cumulative and deserves patience and respect.

MOURN INSIDE OUT

I'll mourn your loss from the inside out.

Grief is a personal journey. Don't let the world determine what yours should look like. You lost a dear pet, a beloved companion.

Grieve their absence on your terms — not anyone else's. Choose to confide in those who respect and honor your grief as you work through it from the inside out.

LIGHT IN THE DARK

I will let your memory light my darkest days.

Even though they are no longer here, your dear cat fills your heart and lights your days through the memories you share. As you grieve, your memories may trigger sadness and pain.

Let them. In time, these memories will be treasures of light that will illuminate the darkest days of your life.

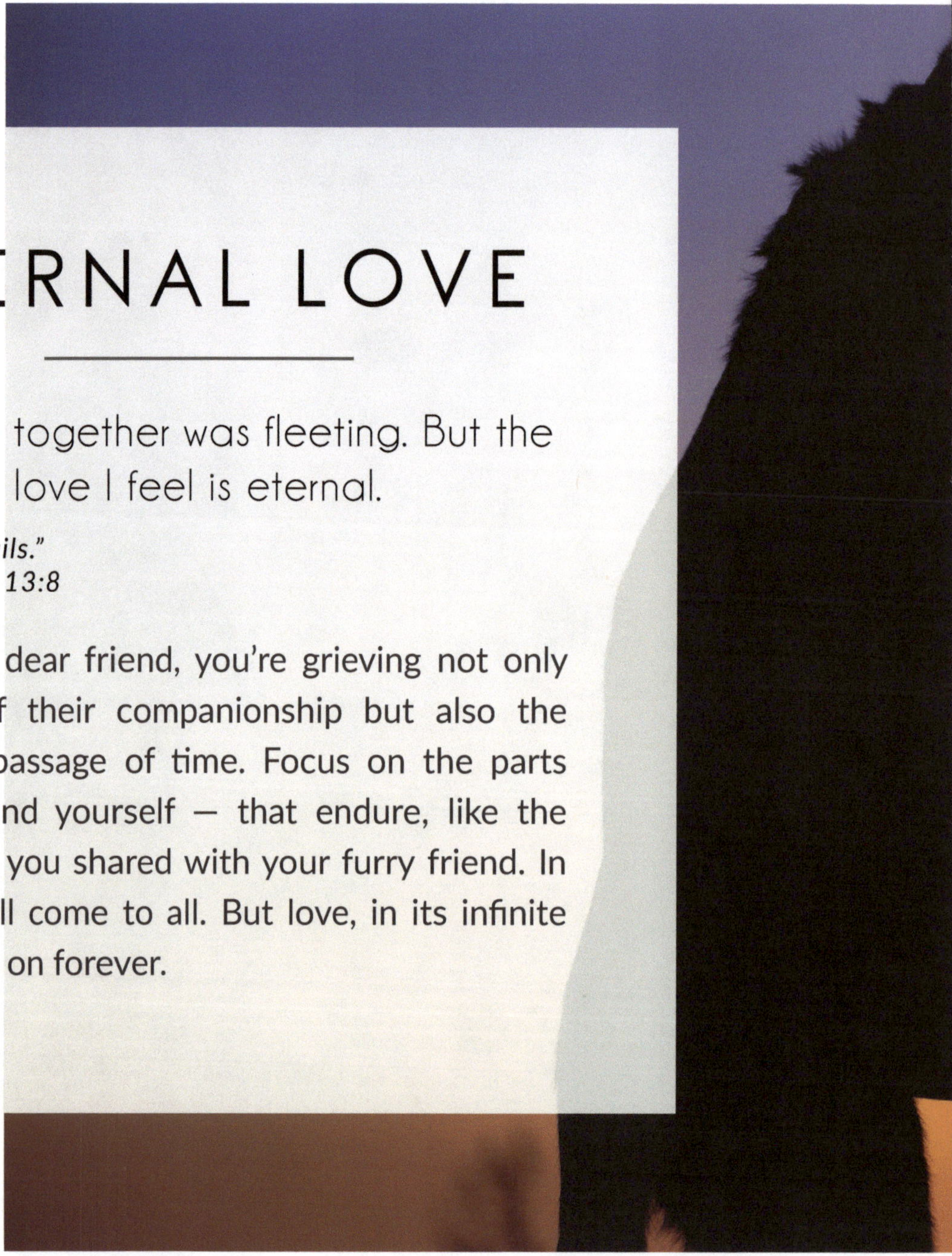

ETERNAL LOVE

Our time together was fleeting. But the love I feel is eternal.

"Love never fails."
1 Corinthians 13:8

In losing a dear friend, you're grieving not only the loss of their companionship but also the inevitable passage of time. Focus on the parts of life — and yourself — that endure, like the connection you shared with your furry friend. In life, loss will come to all. But love, in its infinite magic, lives on forever.

KRISTI HUGSTAD

After her husband's suicide, Kristi Hugstad gained a strong desire to help people who are suffering with grief. This led her to become a certified Grief Recovery Specialist, and her work has helped countless people through the most difficult times in their lives. Through her work, she hopes to help people who have experienced tragic events to gain a new perspective, strengthen their relationship with God, and renew their lives.

Author of "What I Wish I'd Known: Finding Your Way Through The Tunnel of Grief," "Beneath the Surface: A Teen's Guide to Reaching Out When You or Your Friend Is in Crisis," "Be You, Only Better: Real-Life Self-Care for Young Adults (and Everyone Else)," and the "Returning to Joy" series, Kristi shares her personal experience and professional expertise in grief recovery in many ways. In addition to writing books, she is a grief and self-care expert for CBS, professional speaker, contributor for the Huffington Post and Elephant Journal, and is the host of a podcast called "The Grief Girl."

In loving memory of the cats who stole the hearts of my family and friends.

SPECIAL THANKS

Sheila Peterson, Beachside Books | For always believing in me

Juliet Ekinaka, Lunations, Inc | For bringing my vision to life

Kristen Price, Editor | For your creative inspiration

Kika Dorsey, Editor | For your creative inspiration

Val Hugstad, Editor & Support | For always being there

Viki Hugstad, Editor & Support | For always being there

Jeff Campbell, Editor | For all your hard work

Tom Dean, Morgan James | For believing in my mission

CPSIA information can be obtained
at www.ICGtesting.com
Printed in the USA
LVHW071508290721
694054LV00002B/13

* 9 7 8 1 6 3 1 9 5 4 2 1 4 *